A 10 STEP GUIDE TO LINKEDIN PERSONAL BRANDING

DHINESHBABU PERUMAL SAMY

A 10 Step Guide to LinkedIn Personal Branding

A personal brand is the best tool to build your network of peoples which will be a great catalyst in one's career/ professional journey. So, let's do it at the right place!

- Dhineshbabu Perumal Samy (Dariusdnu).

Contents

Foreword

About The Author:

Dhineshbabu was born in 1998 in Tamil Nadu, India. Growing up, he was fascinated with writing, and this interest led to some early exposure to scribbling his thoughts. Later, Mr. Dhineshbabu, who now works as a Digital Marketer, developed a passion for writing. In The Realm of Possibility, Dhineshbabu started publishing his writings on a digital platform with his pen name, Dariusdnu. He has also contributed to many anthologies as a co-author.

Preface

I, Dhineshbabu Perumal Samy (Dariusdnu), the author of this book strongly believe the quote, "Your Network Is Your Net Worth" by Porter Gale and that's why I started to explore networking and finally landed in Personal Branding, When I was looking for a suitable platform to build my brand, I found LinkedIn as it acted as a catalyst for both, my career and personal growth!

So, I wrote this book to share my learnings and let everyone enjoy this wonder.

Acknowledgements

Thank You, Kaushik Kannan and Hari Kumaran for helping me explore this great platform (LinkedIn). My friends (Akshayraj, Nihal Ahamed, Mehraj, Ramesh Kumar) and my parents (Perumal Samy and Ganga Mani) for motivating me to write this book. Last but not least a special thanks to My Friend Nirmal for this fascinating cover design!

Table of Contents

Table of Contents

Introduction

Branding is an act of building a brand for a business and Personal Branding is an act of building a brand for yourself(Personal). LinkedIn is a professional social media platform, where one can connect with business professionals from entry level to C-Level. So, LinkedIn is the best place to build a professional network.

Building a personal brand on LinkedIn helps you in career growth and will also be a great support if you are on/ starting a entrepreneurial journey.

So here, let's look through 10 pro tips that can help you in building your personal brand and make effective use of LinkedIn.

CHAPTER ONE

Add Picture and A Tagline

- As we all know, the first impression is the best impression. The profile picture and the tagline are the elements which someone sees even before visiting our LinkedIn profile.
- Your profile picture may be professional or unprofessional but a headshot picture is much preferable.
- When coming to tagline you can have it in (Designation | Keyword | offer/service) this format.
- Also add a detailed cover picture, that showcases your work and contact.

CHAPTER TWO

Add A Short Description

- Once someone visits your LinkedIn profile the second thing they look at next your picture and tagline is your About Section.

- So it is necessary to have a short and detailed self description in the about section.

- Having a description about your Tagline is advisable.

- You can also add/mention other handles where people can find your work.

CHAPTER THREE

Add Relevant Skills And Achievements

- Your skills and achievements are the key elements that let others (profile visitors) know about the areas of your interests and expertise.

- So add your relevant skills and achievements in their respective sections.

- Avoid adding irrelevant data just to make your profile look fancy.

- Irrelevant data may misguide or make a bad impression on you, when the truth is revealed.

CHAPTER FOUR

POST OFTEN AND PROVIDE VALUE

- Consistency plays a vital role when it comes to social media. Yes, maintaining a consistency in posting shows people and algorithms that you are active and updated. So, post a minimum of three times a week.

- Also, select a niche to which you want to be known for and post/speak more about it.

- At the same time, don't forget to ensure that you provide some value to your readers/visitor/audience.

- Providing Value is very important because though social media works on algorithms, the consumers/end users are humans.

- To say simple, Post for the people and not for the algorithm!

CHAPTER FIVE

Unique Hashtag

- You can create a unique hashtag for yourself and include it in all your posts.

- It helps people to find your posts in a single place other than your profile.

- If you are a person who posts on more than one topic, then you can create a unique hashtag for each topic and segment your audience.

- An audience who is interested in your specific topic posts can follow that specific hashtag and receive your updates instantly on their newsfeed.

CHAPTER SIX

MAKE SURE YOU FEATURE

- Don't forget to make use of the Featured Section in your profile.

- The featured section is a stage to showcase your best works(Posts).

- Highlighting your best pieces attracts more people and let's them know your knowledge and understanding of the topic.

- It may even help you in bringing better engagement and building a niche audience.

CHAPTER SEVEN

Don't Forget To Like and Comment

- What goes out, comes back. Yes, the law of karma is what keeps social media running.
- So, go through your connections posts in your news feed, and react to the posts you like.
- Consuming others' content may help you in generating new content ideas.
- Also, Comment your views on those posts you like/ react to in sentences (one or two lines).
- Make sure you tag the post author when you comment.

CHAPTER EIGHT

Respond To Comments

- We know that replying to comments is always a task, but never fail to respond to comments.
- It helps in creating a better relationship with your fellow creators and your audience.
- Don't forget to take a minimum time gap to respond to the comments you receive.
- Never miss to tag the person who commented on your post, when you reply to the comments you get for your post.

CHAPTER NINE

GIVE AND RECEIVE E & R

- (E) Endorsement and (R) Recommendation are one among the key elements of any LinkedIn Profile.
- The Skills & endorsements section let's others know your skill set and allows your colleagues to endorse you for your skillset which they notice in you just by making a click.
- The Recommendation Section is a place for testimonials from your colleague or client.
- The Endorsement and recommendation adds value to your profile by showcasing your value and helps your profile stand out of the crowd.

CHAPTER TEN

BREAK THE ICE

- Many always have trouble when it comes to speaking with strangers.
- So, with any hesitation you, be the one who breaks the silence and starts speaking (message).
- If Possible create a 2 line self intro and share it with your new connection within one week from the day you got connected.
- You can also break the ice by greeting your connections on their birthdays, work anniversaries and other achievements.

CHAPTER ELEVEN

BONUS - LINKEDIN LIMITATIONS

Here, I'm listing a few limits which are to be followed while using LinkedIn to avoid account being restricted/blocked,

- 60 to 80 messages per day for new accounts and 80 to 100 messages per day for old accounts.
- 25 connection requests per day for new accounts and 70 to 90 connection requests per day for old accounts.
- 30 searches for new/rare used accounts and 300 searches for old/frequently used accounts.

(P.S: These limitations may vary based on conditions)

Personal Branding

Personal Branding is nothing but more of relationship building mixed with some marketing and sales!

Let's Get Connected And Grow Together!

Do you have any feedback or want to discuss with the author about personal branding/marketing/any new ideas?

Then you can connect without any hesitation in any one of the below channels.

- Website: https://www.dariusdnu.com
- LinkedIn: https://www.linkedin.com/in/dariusdnu/
- Instagram: https://instagram.com/dariusdnu
- Twitter: https://twitter.com/dariusdnu
- Facebook: https://www.facebook.com/dariusdnu
- Email: dariusdnu@gmail.com

9 798886 297775

Printed by Libri Plureos GmbH in Hamburg, Germany